A

of a
STAGECOACH ROBBER

The Saga of
Reimund Holzhey,
the Midwest's
Last Stagecoach Robber

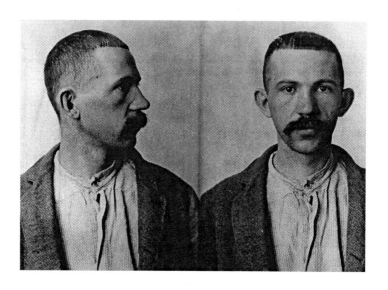

By Bruce K. Cox

Bruce K Cox

Cover: Mug shot of Reimund Holzhey, courtesy of Superior View, Marquette, Michigan.
Cover concept and artwork by John DeMario.

First published by Dog Ear Publishing
4010 W. 86th Street, Ste H
Indianapolis, IN 46268
www.dogearpublishing.net

ISBN: 978-159858-346-5

This book is printed on acid-free paper.
This book is a work of NonFiction.

Printed in the United States of America

Preface

This is a work of creative non-fiction based on the true story of the celebrated highwayman, Reimund Holzhey, who robbed a stagecoach on Stage-coach road between the south end of lake Gogebic and Gogebic Station, Michigan, on August 26, 1889. The story is drawn from contemporary newspaper reports published in various parts of the Midwest, as well as other sources, and is as true to life as possible. Only after reading and studying many articles have I been able to attempt to separate fact from fiction. This is said to have been the last stagecoach robbery east of the Mississippi river. Newspapers called him Rhein-hardt, Reinbold, Redmond, and variations of those names; his surname was often given as Holzhay.

At the time of his brief career as a desperado Holzhey claimed to be suffering from insanity, marked by "spells" when he had violent urges to put himself in danger and completely forgot what he was doing. Holzhey was captured several days after holding up a stagecoach on what is now known as

Stagecoach road. He was taken to Bessemer and locked in the county jail for two months before being placed on trial for first-degree murder and sentenced to two life terms in prison. His mental state declined while in prison and he underwent an operation on his brain a few years after being taken to Marquette. From then on he made a remarkable recovery and became an erudite and polished writer. He made friends with influential people and was pardoned by the governor in 1913.

A description of Holzhey's physical characteristics and personality may be of interest to the reader. He was five feet six and one-quarter inches tall, had light hazel eyes and a blond mustache. His hair was light brown, sandy, and his complexion light to ruddy. Holzhey spoke with a heavy German accent. During his trial in 1889 he appeared to some to display the "serene indifference of a disinterested spectator." Another report said he "never broke down nor manifested the slightest emotion", though other accounts claimed his composure "gave away under cross-examination and he sobbed uncontrollably." At his sentencing he "broke down and seemed dazed."

By 1899 he was called "the best-behaved convict in the prison." By the time of his release he had become "a zealous toiler for self-improvement" and gained "a store of well digested knowledge that would be notable in a thoroughly read college man." Holzhey had "an extensive and well-chosen vocabulary... and an unusual facility in writing." He was taciturn, his "nature naturally shy and retiring." He had a good sense of humor and would laugh "hee hee hee." Holzhey liked children, smoked a pipe and could recite long passages of Shakespeare's plays from memory.

Holzhey denied ever having been a sweetheart of Lillie Rose Huntley, and doubted that he had fired the shots that killed Adolph Fleischbein. During and after Holzhey's jailing and trial in Bessemer various *allegations* of murder were published in the newspapers. It was *claimed* he may have killed somebody out in Montana, and that after he returned to Wisconsin he never sat with his back to a door. A man in Wisconsin told a newspaper that he was sure Holzhey had murdered and robbed a fellow worker down there. A person who knew Holzhey in Marquette county following his release from prison said that he was always the last in line when they hiked through the woods; was this because he lived in fear of retribution and being shot in the back by an avenger of Adolph Fleischbein or some other victim, or is this just more mythology?

Holzhey's remains were cremated after his death, and the ashes spread out on the water between Fort Myers and Captiva Beach.

The author would like to thank Arlene Schneller of Snow Country Real Estate for the use of her extensive collection of newspaper and magazine articles relating to Holzhey and the stagecoach robbery, and John DeMario for designing the cover and scanning some of the illustrations used in this book.

Bruce K. Cox

Holzhey Hill on Stagecoach road,
south of lake Gogebic.

Autobiography of a Stagecoach Robber

From Germany to Fort Howard

My name is Reimund Holzhey. I have lived a long life. Once upon a time I was known as Black Bart, stagecoach robber, but today I am just a sick old man trying to live out the final days of his life. When I look back over the years I have mixed emotions. I had a normal childhood back in Germany, but in later life, plagued by a mental condition caused by an injury to my skull, I took the wrong path and carried out a brief and misguided career as a "desperado." Now, I don't have much time left to tell my story, but I will make the attempt nevertheless.

I was born at Reinschutz, near the town of Schwarzburg, in the region of Thuringia, in the German Duchy of Saxe-Meiningen, on October 2, 1866.

Two weeks before my birth Duke Bernhard was forced to abdicate for siding with the Austrian Emperor Franz Joseph I during the time of troubles between Prussia and Austria. Duke Bernhard II was succeeded by his son, Duke Georg II.

The things I still remember from my childhood back in Germany include the beautiful forest and mountains near my hometown, my father's farm, and my school days. I was a bit of a dreamer during my youth, and often daydreamed about life in the Wild West of America. I sought out whatever books I could find about America, and managed to acquire some written by James Fenimore Cooper. His *Leather Stocking Tales*, with their stories of the noble red man, intrigued and inspired me with an urge to go to the United States and see the country for myself.

My Uncle Christian Schwarz, a wealthy sawmill owner and manufacturer in Fort Howard, had written and invited his nephews to come to work for him; there wasn't much of a future for us in Germany. I had no desire to be a farmer for the rest of my days, so I decided to leave for America; America fever! In 1882, when I was fifteen years old and out of school, I bid auf Wiedersehen to my parents, sisters and friends. All of my worldly goods were packed into a cloth sack. My kinsman, Oscar Werner, accompanied me on the trip.

We traveled to the port of Bremerhaven, where I saw hundreds of people waiting on the Columbus dock before they left Germany. There we boarded the passenger and cargo steamship *Braunschweig*, bound for America. We only had a few thalers, barely enough to pay for steerage class tickets at the North German Lloyd Line office. The ship was loaded with cargo and passengers, and we left the land of our birth.

The trip across the ocean took almost three weeks. All I had to eat were a few boxes of crackers, some sausages and watery soup, and a small ration of water, which was doled out by the sailors aboard the ship. The rolling ocean did not agree with me, and I was thankful when we spotted the American coast-line slowly coming into view. Soon we were berthed in a bustling port in the biggest city in the United States. I still remember the date we arrived there: May 26, 1882.

Before I left home my father gave me an American ten-dollar gold piece with which I was to pay my train fare and expenses from New York to Wisconsin. I kept this coin carefully wrapped up inside a hand-kerchief, which I hid inside my coat. I was told that I would need to show it to the man at the immigration office after reaching America; the Americans did not allow people to enter the country unless one had some money with which to support himself!

At long last we arrived in Fort Howard and were united with Uncle Chris Schwarz, my mother's brother. Uncle Chris had come to America in 1852 with his good friend John Voigt. They built a big sawmill on the Fox river in Fort Howard and became prosperous businessmen. Uncle Chris gave me a job at the mill, working on the planing mill, and I piled boards and learned to operate and maintain the planer and matcher.

I was determined to learn as much as possible about the operation of the sawmill in order to be in a position to take it over someday, should my uncle ever retire from business. This was in 1883. My cousin was a joiner at the factory. I discovered I had a talent for repairing the machinery. Whenever it broke down I was allowed to work on it and get everything in working order again.

It was not long before I learned how to speak, read and write English. There was a saloon near my uncle's home, and I sometimes stopped there to drink a glass of beer and read the newspapers. Once I had mastered the English language I began purchasing dime novels, referred to back in those days as yellow-backed novels. They were sensational stories about outlaws like Jesse James, Black Bart and Billy the Kid. Before long I had a collection of almost 400 of these little books. They inspired me with ideas of adventure, and in 1885 I decided to set out and seek my fortune in the wilds of the North Country. I felt my cousin, being a few years older than me, had a better chance of advancement in Uncle Chris's mill.

The newspapers were then full of stories about the Gogebic iron range and fortunes being made there, so I hopped a train and rode up to Hurley. I took along a Winchester rifle and some camping supplies. Working deep inside the earth didn't appeal to my senses, so I spent most of my time fishing and hunting for wild game in the forests that surround the mining towns. Whenever I needed some money I found employment at one of the local sawmills, but soon grew tired of this life. I went back to my uncle's place in Fort Howard and after a short time decided to seek greener pastures.

My Uncle Oscar Schwarz and Aunt Louisa lived in the little village of Pulcifer, in Shawano county, north of Fort Howard. Uncle Oscar was in business with a man named Bergner, and they operated a gristmill on the Oconto river. I worked in Uncle Oscar's mill for almost two years, until the spring of 1887, when the urge for excitement once again prompted me to seek my destiny.

A Western Adventure
and Disaster

I had read about the 'Wild West' in dime novels and always wanted to see it for myself, so I packed my few clothes into a sack and set out for the Washington territory. There I lived the life of the cowboy, working on a ranch and learning how to fire a six-shooter. I saw Portland, Oregon, travelled to the Puget sound, and worked in a sawmill for a few months. At times I was forced to depend on wild game for sustenance. I owned a horse and a .44 caliber bulldog revolver and made my own knife from an old saw blade.

I killed a deer one day and prepared several meals from it. From part of the hide I managed to make a buckskin sheath for my knife. While I was out west my horse had slipped and fallen on me and injured my head. It was hours before I regained consciousness. I began to suffer from insomnia and melancholia, and had no friends there to care for me or listen to my complaints, so I had no choice but to write home and ask for money to return to Wisconsin.

Uncle Oscar sent me enough money to pay for a train ticket back to Pulcifer in the fall of 1887. That winter I secured employment working in the woods as a scaler. My employer had faith in me and had me cruise the woods along the Oconto river to locate good stands of timber. Summertime was a slow season for me, when I enjoyed the opportunity to hunt and fish but made very little money. I was having spells, after which I couldn't remember anything that had happened.

Sometimes I had hallucinations and felt violent urges come over me. Whenever this happened I tried to head for the woods in order to prevent myself from getting into trouble. I went to Green Bay to see Doctor Palmer about my injury and found that there was very little he could do to help me. This situation did not set well with Uncle Oscar, and I tried to explain to him that I was not feeling well.

When winter came again I was back to work in the woods, scaling timber. This occupation grew tiring, and finally I could stand it no longer, throwing in the towel in February 1889. I told my employer I was tired of working in the woods, and went back to Pulcifer. In the spring of 1889 I decided to go see a doctor in Chicago. He told me there was little he could do to help me, and that I would have to get along as best I could. Uncle Oscar didn't believe there was anything wrong with me; he presented me with an ultimatum: either go back to work or move out of his house.

A Highway Robber's Career

I no longer felt like the person I was before the accident. Frustrated and laboring under a powerful urge to commit violent deeds, I had to survive somehow. That was when I embarked on the life of an outlaw. As I recall, I think I carried out about a dozen robberies in all, although I was credited with many more, as well as some murders!

That spring, sometime in April or May of 1889, I hid in the woods alongside the road between Pulcifer and Simond and waited for the stagecoach to come by. Wearing a red handkerchief over my face, I shouted to the driver to stop, but he kept going. I took a shot at one of the horses with my Winchester and took a bead on the passengers. This finally convinced the driver to obey my orders. As I recall, the people on the stage were almost broke, and I rounded up no more than a few dollars, if anything.

I headed for Green Bay in order to escape any posse that may have been organized to look for me, and spent several days loafing around there and planning my next job. A few weeks later I tried this act again on another stagecoach, and collected close to $100 from two passengers and the mail pouch. Then I waylaid a stockman near Gillett but discovered he had no money. I bumped into another man near Maple Valley who was equally broke.

Towards the end of May I held up the stagecoach coming down the Military road from Shawano. This took place at the Log Cabin on the Wolf river, between Shawano and Langlade. I got about $20, which was about a month's wages in those days, and some mailbags. This success impelled me to try robbing some more stagecoaches, but the results didn't suit me. I stopped the stage near Ellis Junction on the Milwaukee & Northern railway line.

About an hour later I tried my hand at train robbing and got aboard the Milwaukee & Northern train in Maple Valley. After eyeing up the clientele, I waited for the train to get far enough out of town. Then I ordered the brakeman to hand over his valuables and to walk in front of me. He was afraid I was going to shoot him but I reassured him that I would not as long as he behaved himself. The train was full of Italians. They donated $50 and a few cheap watches. Then I pulled the cord and got off near Ellis Junction, a little burg in the middle of nowhere.

Of course, one thing I learned during my outlaw career was that a lone highwayman is at a distinct disadvantage over a gang of men. Because I always needed to hold a gun in one hand, I couldn't search people for their money and valuables; I was completely dependent upon their honesty to hand it over to me.

After robbing the stage I walked through the woods back to Keshena and ran into an old Indian named Honest John on the way. I pulled out my gun and ordered him to hand over his money; he was almost scared to death. I searched his pockets and came up with three pennies, but feeling sorry for the man, I handed them back. Another gentleman donated a few more dollars to my fund.

I played a good joke on the men who formed a posse to track me down. I got into the crowd and rode with them to Bonduel, where I spent the evening in a saloon listening to the talk about the highwayman. There was a Jewish merchant in Bonduel named Solomon Kahn who ran a little store there and had a safe behind the counter. While I was in the saloon I overheard him boasting about being too smart for the stagecoach robber. He told a group of men that I would never be able to rob him!

Now I am ashamed to relate what I did, but back then I was a different, desperate man. The next morning I went over to Mr. Kahn's store and found him standing outside the entrance. I told him I needed to speak to him inside and we went into the store. Then I pulled a gun on him and told him that I was the man who robbed trains, and that I wanted all of his money.

He laughed at me and thought I was joking, then took another look at my gun and decided he better go along with my demands. He forked over $80 and his gold watch. I made him come outside and cut the halters on a team of horses hitched to a post. Then I got up into the seat and rode away as the owner came running down the street. I turned around and fired a couple of shots over his head to settle him down a bit. A few miles outside of town I abandoned the wagon on the road and returned to my camp by foot.

In the wee hours of an August night I boarded a Wisconsin Central train at Abbotsford and waited for it to get a few miles outside of town. When it was far enough out I ran over and opened the sleeping car door. I met the porter and conductor and ordered them to fork over their money and watches.

The porter took off running down the aisle to the sleeping quarters, shouting to the passengers. I fired some shots over his head and soon had him quieted down. I think they donated about $50 and several pocket watches this time. After everything was done I pulled the cord to stop the train and stepped off into the woods near Cadott. This little stunt created quite a sensation in the neighborhood and helped to fuel my outlaw ego.

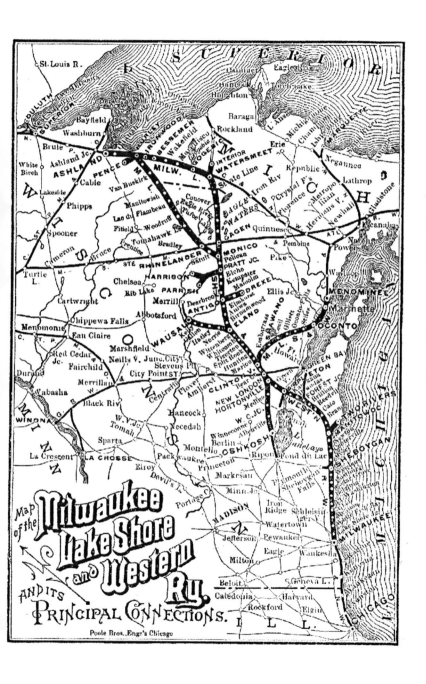

Robbery of the Gogebic Stagecoach

Things were getting pretty hot in the Shawano country in August of 1889, so I decided to head for the Gogebic range. I was familiar with that country from my travels a few years earlier. I took the train to Gogebic Station and rode the stage up to the foot of lake Gogebic, where the railroad company had a big resort. Many wealthy men from the cities came there to fish for black bass, and I knew they might be persuaded to donate to my cause. I became a guide and met some good prospects. While there I boarded at Gogebic Station and took my meals with Theodore Damuth, the stagecoach driver.

The resort assigned a boat to me and I took some men out onto the lake. Adolph Fleischbein, a lawman, was from Belleville, Illinois, and I think Robert Rintoul, Donald Mackerchar, and William Paddon were from Chicago. In the course of conversation I discovered the latter were all bankers, apt to be carrying some cash in their wallets.

Another time I guided two lads, Russell and George Kilbourne, sons of a prominent businessman from Columbus, Ohio, out on the lake. When we returned to shore I took them for a tramp into the woods. The boys were afraid of getting lost but I reassured them. While in the woods I gave them a demonstration of my shooting ability, spotting a porcupine up in a tree and knocking it down with a single shot. We returned to the resort, and I left for Gogebic Station without collecting my pay.

The following day I purchased some provisions and studied a map in the depot. I told everybody that I was going hunting in the woods; I really wanted to hold up the stage, which was nothing more than a lumber wagon, when it came down to the station on Sunday night. After walking up the road a few miles, to the top of a hill, I made a camp in the woods alongside the road. I knew the stagecoach would come by with a group of men returning to Gogebic Station, but it was too dark by the time the stage came by, and I had to abandon the attempt for then.

About ten o'clock in the morning of August 26th I heard the wagon coming up the hill. I walked out to the road just as it was approaching, stood in front of the coach and hailed Damuth. He stopped and asked me if I wanted a ride. I stood with my arms behind my back, holding a revolver in each hand.

"You folks will have to take up a little collection for me this morning," I told them.

Mackerchar, who was seated in back of the wagon, chuckled and asked me how much I wanted.

*The hotel at the resort built by the Milwaukee,
Lake Shore & Western Railway on the south shore
of the lake was called the Gogebic House in 1889.*

I told him, "I will take five hundred dollars," and
showed him my guns. Then something quite unexpected happened. He said, "all right, here's mine,"
and reached inside his coat, pulled out a gun and
began shooting at me. I let loose with both revolvers
from several feet away and two of my shots hit him.

As this was going on, Fleischbein, who was sitting alongside Damuth, stood up to disembark from the wagon. Two of Mackerchar's bullets struck Fleischbein in the right hip; Fleischbein fell off the seat onto the roadway as the team of horses bolted down the road with the wagon. I was too crazed at the time to realize what had happened, but suffice to say my revolvers were .38 and .44 calibers and the bullets removed from Fleischbein's wounds were—I was later informed—.32 caliber, the same as those in Mackerchar's gun! The newspapers reported five shots were fired, though some claimed I shot at the wagon as it departed.

Fleischbein asked me, "Why did you shoot me? Couldn't you see my hands were up?"

I told him, "I'm not going to hurt you. If that other damn fool had kept still, no one would have been hurt!" I couldn't walk away empty handed, so I took Fleischbein's watch and his wallet, which held $37 in cash. As I learned later, Fleischbein had lain on the road for three hours before somebody came back to get him; he died the next morning at the Gogebic Hospital in Bessemer from loss of blood.

Telegraph wires heated up, word of the robbery got out and a posse was formed. The county sheriff, Dave Foley, secured a posse of Indians and dogs from Watersmeet and searched the woods for me. I later learned those so-called "bloodhounds" walked right past my provisions without taking any notice! On several occasions I heard the baying of the dogs but kept far enough ahead of them to escape.

I headed east towards the south branch of the Ontonagon river, thirty miles, where I finally got them off my trail by walking in the river for a few miles. I walked through the woods for three days before reaching the South Shore tracks. All I had to eat were a few crackers in my pocket, wild berries and some meager offerings given to me by homesteaders along the way. I reached a little townsite that was going up about fifty miles west of Nestoria and hopped a train to Champion, where I got off and walked the rest of the way to Republic.

Capture
in Republic, Michigan

About six o'clock in the evening of August 30th I reached the little mossback town of Republic and found lodging at the Republic Hotel. I signed the register as "Henry Plant," had my first good meal in almost a week, and went up to my room. Little did I know that the proprietor, Mr. O'Brien, had recognized me and alerted the local lawmen.

The next morning I got out of bed at 6 o'clock, went downstairs for breakfast, paid my bill and walked out the door. As far as I could tell I was in the clear and about to continue my escape back to Wisconsin. Two husky men were waiting for me to pass by on the street. Before I knew what was happening one of the men grabbed my arms and told me he was arresting me on suspicion. As I reached inside my coat for a knife the other man knocked me out cold with a billy club.

I was in a groggy state as they half-carried me to

the town hall. When I regained my senses I found myself seated in a chair with my hands handcuffed behind my back. These men were fortunate to have tricked me, as at that time I would have shot both of them dead if given half a chance. The lawmen grilled me incessantly but to no avail, for I refused to reveal my identity and gave evasive answers to all of their inquiries.

A crowd of people was gathered outside shouting, "lynch him!" I shouted back to them, "Come and get me you brave boys! I would rather be strung up or shot dead than handcuffed to this chair!" At the time I didn't know if I was headed for the gallows or the nearest tree.

While I was being held in the town hall my captors, Marshal John Glade and Deputy Pat Whelan, took me to a photographer named Taylor and had their picture taken standing either side of me, their trophy. These photographs were then hawked to eager souvenir seekers. I must confess, this made me feel more important than I should have. But back then I was suffering from a mental condition that severely impaired my moral faculties.

The men who captured me had quite an argument over who was going to receive the $5,000 reward, and were reluctant to turn me over until this point was settled. At noon I was placed aboard a train and taken to the county jail in Marquette. Large crowds stood along the tracks at every town along the route. When the train pulled into Ishpeming, I stood by a window and made a sweeping bow to the people assembled there.

Courtesy of Bentley Historical Society,
University of Michigan, Ann Arbor.

At the county jail in Marquette, I stretched out on a bed in the jail cell. Soon after my incarceration a reporter was brought to my cell and asked, "Are you Reimund Holzhey?"

"I don't know. You ought to know."

"Are you the man who held up the stage?"

I replied, "Ya. I guess so."

Within a day or two the sheriff and thirteen other men came over from Bessemer. Theodore Damuth was among them. I asked him, "Were you hurt?"

He replied, "No."

"Well, you're damn lucky" I told him.

Incarceration in the Gogebic County Jail

They took me back to the Gogebic county seat aboard a South Shore train. We came in from the north of town instead of going to the depot in Bessemer, thus missing the crowd at the railroad depot who had wanted to hold a lynching bee for me. The county jail was still under construction and lacked a roof over it. I was locked up with some other prisoners inside a little room in a corner of a little wooden cracker-box on the courthouse grounds. The sheriff slept in the jail that night and went out and hired two guards the next day.

The following evening a group of young women came to see me. They climbed up onto a woodpile in the next lot and hollered over the fence, "Reimund, we want to talk to you!"

I answered, "What do you want?"

They replied, "Us girls came to get a look at you."

"Are you glad to see me?" I asked. One of my companions held up the lamp behind my head so the girls could see me.

They all shouted, "Yes!"

"Do you want me to come out and see you?" I rattled the grate on the window as if I was going to remove it. This frightened them, and one of the girls almost fell off the woodpile. "Don't be afraid, I'm not going to hurt you. I'll get out of here before long and come to see you. They can't keep me in here much longer. Good-night!" The next day Foley clamped a ball-and-chain around my ankle just in case.

Sheriff Foley told a newspaper that I had told him he could not keep me for long and that I would never be captured alive once I escaped. A few days later the new sandstone jailhouse was ready, and I moved into new quarters; the ball-and-chain was removed from my ankle. One of my fellow inmates was a man named Garrett Burns. He had been an accomplice of two other men in the burglary of a saloon in Watersmeet earlier that summer. They stole about ten dollars in change from a till, entering and exiting through a broken window.

Burns was given instructions to grill me for any incriminating information he could possibly draw from me. In order to accomplish this he told me he was going to interview me and write my life's story. Of course, he came up with some very imaginative tales that bore little semblance to reality. He claimed I had committed no fewer than nineteen robberies, as well as several murders.

The boys locked up in jail with me wanted to know how I got the nickname Black Bart. I explained to them that I had never seen that moniker attached to my name before it was published in a Duluth newspaper following the Gogebic stagecoach robbery. The newspaper simply reported that my exploits rivaled those of Black Bart in California.

The Huntleys
of Hartland, Wisconsin

I had no confidants or friends to help me at that time, but the newspapers claimed I had a girl-friend named Rose Huntley who lived with her parents in a little town called Hartland, between Shawano and Green Bay. I was acquainted with Mr. and Mrs. Huntley and their daughters Lillie and Carrie. Carrie Huntley was about fourteen years old and her sister Lillie Rose was about eighteen.

During some of my tramps in the Shawano country I had been by the Huntley home and entertained the family with my six-shooters. Henry Huntley allowed me to sleep in his barn. He had some hickory trees growing on his property and I would pick up a few nuts, throw them into the air and shoot at them. Sometimes I had his daughters toss them up. This always seemed to impress the girls.

They had a little brother named George who was about fifteen years old. Whenever I stopped by their farm he wanted to see my revolvers and do some target shooting. We had a few competitions, but I always out-shot him. Sometimes I rode around a tree in the yard and fired at a target from horseback. There were few entertainments in those times and parts, so the Huntleys enjoyed my visits.

Henry Huntley had moved there from Canada. He was a farmer and had a reputation for being somewhat rambunctious. His wife Emily was a Prussian woman, almost twenty years his junior. She had been an early settler in the neighborhood and was one of the Robenhorst girls. The newspapers tried to make one or the other of the Huntley sisters into my girlfriend, even claiming that one of them had accompanied me during some of my robberies! None of this was true.

I had a friend named Kavanaugh who lived about nine miles east of Shawano, near Shawano lake. After my Uncle Oscar kicked me out of his home I went to stay at Kavanaugh's place, which was near the railroad tracks. He worked in the woods while I went about my own business in the neighborhood. I had to be careful because a few people recognized me after my hold-ups and the law was keeping an eye on Kavanaugh's place. The county sheriff and some Pinkertons came around to check on my "hideout" after I held up the Wisconsin Central and the stagecoach in August 1889.

A fool pinkie detective named Harriman went around the neighborhood collecting information on the Huntley family and spread the rumor that Lillie Rose Huntley was my associate in crime. The newspapers loved this story and made her into a regular Annie Oakley; the Huntleys, by some accounts, were an outlaw family! Harriman came to see me in jail and prodded me with this ridiculous story. I told him I had no girl and there was no girl foolish enough to like a fellow like me. The last I ever saw or heard from the Huntleys or Kavanaugh was before I left Shawano county in August of 1889. None of them contacted me after I was captured at Republic.

Some Experiences in Jail

Once again a photographer was brought in to take a photograph of me. Mr. Whitesides came to the county jail and had me pose with a rifle and a vest full of shotgun shells. These souvenir photographs were eagerly sought after by the tourists who came to have a look at the desperado in the Gogebic county jail.

Another of my companions in the jail was a flim-flam man named John Mangus. He had flown into town on a train and walked into a pharmacy in Ironwood where he purchased a ten-cent cigar and paid for it with a ten-dollar gold piece. The proprietor gave him his change, a five dollar gold coin and $4.90 in change. Mangus then pulled his nefarious game and tricked the man into making more change until Mangus walked out with the cigar, his original ten dollar gold coin and an additional five dollar gold piece. That was how he made his living. Mangus was being "put up" to implicate me in various kinds of misbehavior in return for leniency.

The turnkey at the jail was an Irishman named John Ryan. He would bring us our meals and pass them through an opening in the bars on the door. The opening was supposedly just big enough for me to squeeze through if given a chance. Mangus informed the sheriff that I intended to remove a plank from the table in our cell and wait for Ryan to come to pick the plates up off the floor. As he leaned over I would ram the plank through the bars into his head, knock him out and make good my escape.

In the middle of my trial a newspaper report came out claiming that I had tried to bribe the turnkey at the jail with an offer of $1,000 to release me. It was one of my fellow prisoners—probably Mangus—tempted with the offer of his release from jail, who wrote a fake letter, addressed to the sheriff, offering to bribe him with several thousand dollars in return for my release. His trial took place at the same term of court as mine, and he was sentenced to thirty days in the county jail—which he had already served!

A posed photo of the bandit, taken by the Whitesides Studio in Ironwood, Michigan. Collection of the author.

My Trial
in Bessemer, Michigan

A bout two months passed between my capture and the time I was put on trial in Bessemer, charged with first-degree murder in the death of Adolph Fleischbein. My attorneys were Henry Gerpheide of Chicago, Fremont C. Chamberlain and Charles F. Button of Bessemer. My defense was to be based upon insanity and the fact that Fleischbein had been killed by shots from a .32 caliber revolver fired from behind.

My revolvers were .38 and .44 caliber. Many reports appeared in the newspapers just after the robbery stating that Fleischbein's wounds were in his right hip, but Dr. Whiteside testified at the trial that the wounds were in his left hip and two .44 caliber bullets were removed. Fleischbein was already long in the ground and there was nobody to testify in my defense on any of the facts involved.

I was led in shackles to the courthouse. The prosecutor—Charles M. Howell—and Judge Williams were determined to have me locked up for life, and the trial was a mere formality. Howell had told a newspaper reporter that it was a shame there was no capital punishment in Michigan. Another newspaper had tried to stir up a lynching party by publishing an incendiary diatribe against me.

The court had tremendous difficulty in finding twelve jurors who had not already heard of me and formed opinions in regard to my guilt or innocence. I think they went through 700 people before selecting a jury. The newspapers reported me as displaying a serene indifference, but to tell the truth I honestly felt I would be acquitted of the crime of murder.

The jury heard the story of my life and the explanation of why I had done the things that led to my imprisonment and trial. I told them about the accident out West when my horse fell on me, and the subsequent spells that came over me. Nobody was there to testify on my behalf. I told them I had very little recollection of the shooting on the road to Gogebic Station because at the time I was having one of my spells. I didn't recognize Damuth or know the identity of Mr. Fleischbein until sometime later, after I had time to recover my senses.

Fleischbein's bloody clothes were waved in front of the jury to stir them up against me. One of the opposing attorneys wanted to know why I carried two guns when I knew I was subject to spells. I told him I needed to carry them for self-defense as I was frequently out in the wilderness all by myself. To this day I can say that I had the poorest lawyers ever assigned to a man charged with murder!

They didn't bring up a single person to testify in my defense. They actually used the prosecution's witnesses to testify for me! They cross-examined Dr. Whiteside to try to establish my insanity defense, and ranted about me being addicted to dime novels. My lawyer told the jury that I thought I belonged to Texas Jack's gang. It was a poor defense. Needless to say, I had no chance of escaping a life sentence with that sort of legal help.

On the morning of November 16, 1889, I was led over to the courthouse from the jail. The jury was sent out at nine-thirty that morning and returned with their verdict forty-five minutes later: Guilty, sentenced to two life terms in solitary confinement. I couldn't believe it but should have known better. I am told that this farce cost the taxpayers of that county ten thousand dollars. The prosecuting attorney told the newspaper that I had stolen ten thousand dollars during my career as a train and stagecoach robber, but I hadn't stolen even a twentieth as much as that.

Imprisonment
at Marquette, Michigan

Sheriff Foley took me to the state branch prison at Marquette the following day. The prison, which had a sandstone facade and resembled a castle or fortress, had just recently been completed and opened to business. I was registered as prisoner number 37 and placed into a five by seven foot cell where I spent the following twenty-four years of my life. An appeal for a retrial was turned down in February of 1890. At the prison they had free rein to torture me at will, exhibiting me like a wild animal to gawking onlookers and mocking me as I sat inside the cell. My mental condition grew steadily worse.

Later that year I managed to secure a butter knife, which I sharpened by rubbing it back and forth across the masonry. Then one day I took a guard named Palliser hostage and held the knife to his neck. He got away, so I grabbed a fellow prisoner, Richard Meservey. My intent was to provoke one of the guards into shooting me in order to end my suffering, but Warden Tompkins took careful aim with a rifle and shot the knife out of my right hand, along with four of my fingers.

I was placed in solitary confinement on reduced rations. My injured hand added to my misery. My mind continued to deteriorate during this confinement, and I decided it would be best to starve myself to death. I lost almost fifty pounds over the course of a year before the warden took notice and had me whipped with a leather strap. Despite this rough treatment I still refused to eat, and the prison guards resorted to force-feeding me. I was suffering from periodic spells of insanity.

One day I broke a piece of tin off a water pail, sharpened the edge and used it to slit my wrist. A guard spotted me and went to get help. Before he returned I tried to bash my head against the wall of the cell. The warden had me placed into a straight jacket; my spells had become more frequent, and the authorities were finally beginning to believe me. This last suicide attempt was falsely attributed to alleged regret over the recent marriage of Lillie Rose Huntley.

In the summer of 1891 I inquired of Warden Malmgren about the welfare of Fleischbein's widow Luella and family, and whether they were in need. Little did I know that on that very day Fleischbein's sister had visited the prison and viewed me in my cell. A newspaper carried an account of a purported conversation I was said to have had with her, claiming that I had promised to 'do everything in my power to atone for my crime.' This report reached Fleischbein's widow in Illinois, whose bitter reply was, "I would not take a dollar from Holzhey to save my life. I would spurn it as the touch of a viper!"

The Restoration of My Sanity at Ionia, Michigan

I warned the warden that I could feel another powerful spell coming on and was afraid of what I might do to myself or somebody else. The doctor at the prison decided that I was indeed "dangerously insane." In November 1893 I was transferred to the Ionia Asylum in the Lower Peninsula where I underwent trepanning surgery on my skull.

Sometime before my transfer to Ionia and the operation I had prepared a letter to be given to the press in the event of either my death or complete loss of my sanity. The letter was released and published in full by the *Detroit Evening News* a week after my arrival at Ionia. The following is the full text of this letter, given to Warden Malmgren, who deposited it with the newspaper:

Marquette Prison

It is only after long hesitation that I have been able to overcome the dislike of writing to you about myself, for it always recalls to my mind the scenes of folly, misery and falsehood committed by and against me at a time when the darkened faculties of my mind seemed to tremble in the balance between reason and insanity; so that I have tried as much as possible to banish these gloomy recollections. If I recall them once more by writing to you it is not because of any good it could do me, but because I feel as if it was a duty. I owe it to myself to say now that I can see and calmly judge the events of my life and what can be said in my defense.

If I appeal to anything at all it will be to your sense of disinterested justice, where the case must stand or fall by its own merit; for I do not have the means or even the inclination to ever employ a lawyer to distort the facts that might bear on my case as it was done in the so-called fair trial where I was condemned. I shall try to make this statement as short as possible, and I shall only go into those details that are absolutely necessary for a true understanding of the case.

The laws of this country admit that cases may, and do, arise in which persons cannot be regarded as free acting agents, responsible for their actions though such actions prove criminal, and on the supposition that at the time I committed the crimes I am accused of my mind was distressed by causes which I could not control, must rest everything that can be said in my defense.

It is now more than five years since the symptoms of the disorder that brought about my fall manifested themselves. I paid little attention to them for the decay of my physical and mental power was so gradual as not to arouse apprehension, mistaking it for a temporary disorder. But when in time it grew steadily worse I became alarmed and sought medical advice but without relief. I shall not dwell on the details of the physical disorder for, though I suffered intensely, the direct physical pain was nothing compared with the mental distress and irritability which it brought about.

Through lack of nutrition, by indigestion, my nervous system had become so shattered as to deprive me entirely of healthful sleep, for the heavy-eyed wakefulness that took its place was but a continual nightmare. Add to the effects of bad health and the elements of insomnia a well-developed case of melancholia, inherited from the father's side and which had lain latent in me till now, consider this condition as lasting for years without a hope for change for the better, and then tell me how many persons out of a hundred if placed under similar conditions could have saved themselves from becoming either suicides, criminals or outright maniacs.

At the same time it must also be considered that the combined effects of lack of nutrition, insomnia and melancholia produced a direct change in the physical organization of the brain, impairing the memory and entirely paralyzing the higher mental and moral faculties. Even now I can remember how I wondered in a vague way over the change that was taking place in my moral nature, because for some time I had a distinct sensation of emptiness as if something valuable had gone from me, and well I might feel that way, for it was my conscience that had deserted me. After that time I was like a wreck, drifting about without will and judgment to check the evil, but mostly foolish impulses that took possession of me, because so perverted were the moral faculties that acts of folly and meanness I would have scorned to do while in normal condition came to appear to me perfectly right and natural. Where before I had been open-hearted and sociable, I now became suspicious and retiring, motivated by an instinctive impulse that made me conceal my true condition as much as possible.

My friends, and I think I had friends then, noticing the change and judging by outward appearances alone, not comprehending the causes, soon came to draw themselves aloof from me, and the involuntary distrust and aversion which I felt toward human society naturally came to be regarded as surliness and ill-will. Had this change been less abrupt it would have been readily ascribed to ill-health I suffered. But taking place so gradually I came to be regarded as being possessed of a naturally evil disposition.

Of course this state of things could not last forever. That I kept for a long time comparatively straight, was perhaps the result of long-continued good habits and surroundings. But at last the direct strain of the physical disorder, combined with the effects of long-continued brooding over my miserable and hopeless condition , proved too much for the weakened mind. How the impulse that swept away the last feeble safeguards of self-restraint originated in my mind, I am not able to tell, for the impressions of this period on my mind are so confused that I am unable to recall them. Only this much I remember, that where before I had all my thoughts centered on getting well, I was now entirely ruled by the impulse of committing desperate deeds— less to injure anybody than to place myself in situations where I had to expect to be shot down any moment.

Of course, to the sane mind this idea must seem ridiculous, for I myself cannot help now but smile over my own folly. But at that time, and for many months afterwards, the mainspring of all my actions was this one fixed idea. Of course, I am absolutely unable to recall the singular process of reasoning upon which were founded the few but fixed ideas that controlled my actions.

The narrow circle of my thoughts must have been extremely self-centered, my mind being absolutely unable to attach itself to anything but self. The result could not help being a selfishness so intense as to render me utterly heedless of the wrong I might inflict on others. This will also explain my reluctance to speak about myself after I realized my condition, seeing that only by forcing the mind to occupy itself with external objects could I ever hope to prevent it from preying upon itself. I am convinced now that these desperate criminal outbreaks were instinctive efforts of the mind to break away from narrow, self-centered thoughts. The realization of imminent peril would naturally tend to force thought into new channels, giving ease and relief under circumstances which could hardly have been regarded as comfortable by any sane man. I do not think I actually desired to be killed and I am certain I had no desire to kill anybody. The main motive was apparently a keen, irresistible desire for the sensation of danger, as its realization would at least partially dispel the dark mental shadows and tone up the shattered nervous system.

You may also observe that all the crimes committed by me were of a nature tending to stir up intense excitement and sharp universal pursuit, without in the least offering proportional inducement for gain to compensate for the irresponsible chances I took with my life, had the cause of my actions been the love of gold.

When the tension of the nerves caused by the commitment of a desperate deed after a time gave way to reaction and the horrors of mental anguish came back upon me, I dare say it was a natural thing that the action that alone could give relief was repeated again and again. If it had been the love of money which made a criminal out of me, I would surely have taken it at any time I stood a need of it, yet I know I went for weeks and months without it, rather begging or starving, when it would have been an easy matter to supply myself by force. Often when the dark spell was over me it would drive me on for days and nights, either shunning the sight of man by aimlessly wandering through pathless woods till overcome with physical exhaustion or seeking relief in the before described manner. Although at those times I lived more like a wild beast of the woods than a human being, yet I feel sure that the excitement and hardships I endured, restored, at least to some extent, my physical health, and in time might have rectified the mental disorder.

When I was arrested it was the first time that I ever came in contact with the law, and I naturally had not the faintest idea of the methods of what constituted a fair trial. Considering that at that time I could not fully comprehend my condition or see the causes that led up to it, indeed, was entirely unable to form a chain of logical reasoning; you may perhaps perceive what chances for impartial justice I had with an enraged and mis-instructed populace, which was kept in a ferment of excitement by any number of false and exaggerated reports. You remember, perhaps, having read in the papers how friends of mine were moving heaven and earth to get me free by fair means or foul; how my cell was found stocked with all kinds of tools; how I attempted to kill the jailer and escape; and that I really did escape. When in truth, I have never seen nor heard, from some months before I was arrested, until now, of a single one of my former acquaintances; neither did I ever make the faintest attempt to escape; nor were there any tools found in my possession.

Yet those perverted stories could not help giving an unconscious bias to even the highest-minded of my future judges. Nay, the prosecution went so far as to engage two fellow-prisoners, both ex-convicts and professional crooks, to watch my movements, promising speedy release if they could get from me any admission of my guilt, when I don't think the thought of denial ever entered my mind. But to gain their liberty one produced the story of the attempted killing and escape, and the other invented a catalogue of crimes alleged to have been committed by me in states where I had never set foot.

Threats of lynching and other incidents of like nature did not fail to bring about in me that rigidity of nerves which could partly clear my mind and increase powers of self-control. Yet, I was as far removed from my normal self as a corpse animated by electricity is far from a true man. Being kept in this condition during my trial a tolerably clear impression of those proceedings have been left on my memory, and thus enables me, after regaining reasoning power, to see the nature of the justice accorded me.

Imagine for a moment on one side a poor fool without money or friends, an entire stranger in the country, with appearances against him, only gifted with a small amount of slow cunning in certain directions, but without the intelligence and higher reason which might enable him to right himself in the eyes of the world, and you will have a true picture of what I must have been at that time.

Then on the other hand the public prosecutor, with one of the ablest lawyers of the state for assistant, any amount of money to call witnesses and hunt up evidence and supported by a public sentiment that, excited by true and false reports, only saw the effects of the crime, but never for a moment saw the true cause leading to it; the ceremony of the trial could be nothing but a mockery of justice. You may perhaps say that friends of mine engaged a noted lawyer from Chicago to defend me, as had been reported by the papers, and as even myself, swayed by ludicrous impulses of credulity and suspicion, was made to believe. Yet I can see plainly now that these lawyers were engaged either by the sheriff or the prosecution or by both together, for the effect as though everything that money or talent could do was being exerted in my defence.

The truth of this view may be seen by any logical mind that followed the proceedings of my trial. The council for the defense did absolutely nothing but examine about all the jurors that could be found in the county and then address a short speech to the jury selected. But in this way the sheriff was able to realize a big sum by summoning jurors and the prosecuting attorney was entitled to engage an assistant on a fee of $1,000 to help him crush a stillborn defense of an atrocious villain.

As I said, I know next to nothing about legal proceedings, but I think I can show that those who say I had a fair trial are grossly in error.

In the first place, the judge decided against the motion for postponing the trial to the next term of court or of removing it to another county, and yet it cannot be denied that, if there ever was a case where it was necessary to wait till public excitement had somewhat subsided, mine was one of them. The judge came to his decision by asking several parties if they thought they could give me a fair trial according to the evidence, when any intelligent person must realize that these men, if not willing to impeach themselves with unfair dealing, were forced to answer in the affirmative. Yet I would swear that these same men, without, perhaps, being conscious of it, had so firm a conviction of my guilt that even the strongest evidence to the contrary would not have overcome the bias of their minds.

The state had summoned witnesses out of half a dozen different states to testify against me, but did not even attempt to secure the services of a single one of the witnesses proposed by the defense. As the entire defense rested on the supposition that I was suffering through causes beyond my control, with mental aberrations, and consequently irresponsible of action, the entire absence of all who could have thrown any light on that subject naturally made the defense merely nominal. Had I been rational enough to conduct my own defense, the lack of means would have been an effectual bar to securing witnesses that were absolutely necessary. All my physicians and acquaintances, who alone could have observed the change in my mental and physical condition, were living in distant states, and the state's refusal to summon them, together with my inability to call them at my own expense, naturally left me helpless. The witnesses for the state merely testified as to the crime committed, something that had never been denied; but being absolute strangers to all of them, it would have been against all reason to expect these people, biased as they must have been, to have an insight into a mental condition so strange that it might baffle the skill of the most learned.

I have never come much in contact with insane people, but I have read how some of them may not show anything abnormal in their behavior for long periods of time, yet who are always liable to act on the impulse of some one insane idea. My own condition at that time was very much of that nature, but it was only years afterwards that I had sufficiently recovered my balance to understand my own case, as before stated. The feeling of mental distress and the shattered nervous system could only be relieved and stimulated by the realization of a feeling of danger, but how fierce and irresistible this desire was, will be shown later on, when its absence brought over me suffering so intense and agonizing as to reduce me to a condition of imbecility.

Meantime the people, judging from outward appearances alone and seeing me as cool and self-possessed as an iceberg in the most awing situations, without showing the least emotion either of fear or repentance, naturally came to the conclusion that I had reached the acme of cold-blooded villainy, with nerves of steel and heart of stone.

Yet at that time I resembled more a volcano with its lawless forces chilled into a sudden, temporary frigidity than anything else I can think of. As the crimes committed by me created so much of an excitement, it must be they were of an extraordinary nature, and if so, it would not be an unlogical conclusion to ascribe them as the effect of an uncommon cause; the more so as it was less the murder of an innocent man than the extraordinary nature of my exploits which had fastened upon me so much public attention. (I came to this conclusion from the fact that a man who had shot and killed two or three persons when in their sleep, a deed all things considered, surely more atrocious than mine, did not attract half the attention and abuse with which I was overwhelmed.)

It seems characteristic of human nature to ascribe the actions of others to the worst possible motives, and the more corrupt of heart the critic the more scathing will be his judgment. So, following up this rule, the prosecutor concluded that love of gold was the cause of my actions. Now had this been so, a thoughtful mind must have determined that the ruling trait of my character was an avarice almost beyond human conception, combined with a reckless foolishness, equally extreme. Yet both these traits are perhaps more strange to my nature than to most other men, for I never was anxious to accumulate money nor needed it to gratify expensive habits, and I would any day rather go out of my way to avoid a quarrel than seek one.

The other proposition that by the perusal of blood and thunder literature, my imagination had become fired with the ambition of becoming one of the so-called dime novel heroes, would suppose me possessed of aspirations so strange and inconceivable in one of my nature that I cannot give it any serious consideration. I think it would have been an easy matter to establish by competent witnesses that when in my normal condition, avarice, quarrelsome foolhardiness, cruelty or the ambition to shine by these qualities, were the least of my vices. And as by the nature of my crimes they could only have been committed by a sane man, who possessed the above mentioned qualities, one or all to an extraordinary degree, the proof of their absence in me would, at least in the mind of fair-minded and intelligent men, have shaken the very base of the prosecution, which rested entirely on the theory that love of gain was the motive of my actions.

I cannot remember what I said in my defense; it would not have been anything sensible or rational, for how could I, when I could not even half comprehend my own condition, much less explain it to other people. But even if I had been able to do so, my statements, unsupported by a single witness, would not have been regarded with the slightest consideration. Yet I know that by a fair investigation the truth of what I write now could easily have been verified. But the presence of the brothers and the weeping widow of the murdered, a pathetic speech by an able lawyer, with a liberal display of the dead man's bloody clothes, could not fail to impress the jury that I must be a fiend.

But as I had become so against my will it was an act of senseless, inhuman cruelty to punish me with such severity. It could neither undo the injuries inflicted by me or have a restraining influence on the conduct of persons suffering in a similar manner; for how utterly unconscious I was of the fear of human law and retribution is well shown by the fact that not until some time after my arrest did I learn that murderers are not hung in this state.

The mere fact that $10,000 or more were spent for prosecuting, and absolutely nothing for defending me (I do not remember what was done with the few dollars which I had in my possession), the fact that

the state had on hand any number of witnesses while no attempt was made to secure
a single one for the defendant; the fact that
the nominal counsel for the defense did
absolutely nothing to deserve that name
and that the defendant was not in a condition of mind to be able to make his own
defense, and the fact that in a matter where
a man's liberty or life long imprisonment
depended on the correct decision of the
question of responsibility of action, not one
of all the witnesses or people present had
been personally acquainted with the
accused for any length of time, when such
might easily have been secured, will be
enough to show the true nature of my trial.
I cannot think that the proceedings of my
trial would be regarded as legal and just by
an impartial judge, for if this indeed was
human justice, then its opposite could not
be in existence.

After I had been transferred to the state
prison, the nervous tension which at once
concealed and prevented the utter collapse
of my mind, and which through previous
incidents had been brought to the highest
pitch, for a long time aided me in upholding
my self-control by its precarious support.
But it could be but a question of time,
longer or shorter, as the case may be, when
reaction must set in. I dare say, when it did
come, the change would reveal itself in my
features and actions, for I was confined
closer and closer, which of course could not
help but accelerate the catastrophe.

When under the combined influence of insomnia and acute melancholia, multiplied now by enforced physical and mental inactivity, the distress of mind had again absolutely gone beyond endurance, it would indeed have been strange if the impulse for relief should not now possessed me as it had so often done before. If I remember rightly, I tried to compel the officers to shoot me—nothing more nor less. The reason I did not kill myself instead of trying to make others do so, is again explained by the fact that it was less the desire of death than a restless impulse for the sensation of danger. I blame them but not for shooting off my hand—perhaps it had to be done to prevent more serious trouble; but the ingenious cruelty with which I was treated for months afterward would have done credit to fiends. Add to the pain of a shattered hand the torments of melancholia and insomnia which prevented sleep for weeks at a time and the situation might be such as to crush the endurance of the stoutest heart.

But the fact that I, with all my nervous irritability and restlessness, was buried in a space of 5x7 feet, left for months without the least thing to engage a distracted mind, nor being able to modify the nervous restlessness by physical exhaustion, naturally increased my suffering ten-fold. Yet even this was not enough. License was given to everybody, visitors, guards, and prisoners, to mock and abuse me in my hearing to their heart's content, at all times of day or night, and as it was the main feature of my mental trouble that all the thoughts of my mind were concentrated and chained on its own miserable condition, the above mentioned treatment soon so intensified this that I sank into a state of silent stupidity, the mind almost refusing to take or retain outside impressions, but never entirely losing the consciousness of its own condition.

The people of this enlightened and humane age shudder at the tortures inflicted by the savage on his hapless prisoner, but what are the short-lived agonies of a day of physical pain compared with the exquisite suffering of the spirit, that is struggling, for months and years on the brink of an abyss, where not merciful oblivion, but the dark shadows of madness are waiting to engulf him. Yet, as the above-mentioned state is not marked by gaping wounds and torn limbs, the thoughtless and ignorant, unable to comprehend a condition like this, will simply deny its existence, but the few who have passed through similar phases will know that human language can never express what is felt at such times. As long as I was free, physical exhaustion produced by hunger and exercise, together with the stimulus of ever-present danger, had kept me from sinking to the horrors of this last stage, when my mental confusion was often so great that the speech of others seemed a confused, meaningless noise; and the faculty of speech often entirely deserted me. I don't know if this is insanity, but as I had been driven from crime to crime by impulse of preventing the above-mentioned horror from overwhelming me, I will leave it to any fair man to judge if my actions sprung from freewill or were the offspring of causes beyond my control.

At one time, when in a frenzy, I tried to dash out my brains, and was kept in irons for months afterward. It must have been in a brighter moment when I conceived the idea that starvation meant physical exhaustion and physical exhaustion would produce a certain mental relief, or perhaps it was caused by a desire of death—it does not matter which. At least, I remember that by going without food for weeks at a time I would sink into a kind of listless stupor. In this condition of exhaustion I had to keep myself for more than a year; for any time, when by satisfying the craving of hunger, I regained some of my physical strength, the mental distress, perhaps from the pressure of the blood on the brain, would increase to such an extent as would soon again have thrown me into a state of savage frenzy. I will leave it to you to consider what my feelings must have been, when for the purpose of relieving a greater ill, I had to keep myself on the point of starvation for more than a year.

I do not know what sinister and malicious motives were given as causes of my actions at this period, but I dare say it was in the interest of those in authority to make me appear in the worst light possible. It was done without hesitation. As I was still less able at this time than I had been at my trial to explain matters concerning me, I was undoubtedly regarded by the people, judging but from outward appearances and interested one-sided evidence, as a villain so black of heart that no amount of punishment could be too great for me.

I dare say it would be but natural if I should hate them, who, without fairly investigating, so needlessly increased my sufferings. It has been mentioned as evidence of my utter depravity that I never showed the least feeling of repentance and remorse. The explanation is easy enough, for the impressions the crimes committed by me left on my mind are so vague and unreal that they appear to my consciousness more like half-forgotten dreams.

Although I cannot feel violent remorse for my deeds committed while in an abnormal condition, I yet feel truly sorry for them to whom I have been an unwilling cause of suffering and distress. And if any suffering of mine would undo the past or effect any present good, I would be perfectly willing to bear it, because it is contrary to the instincts of my nature that I should have been the means of injury to them that never harmed me. But as no suffering of mine can undo the past, or do good to those I injured, I deny the justice of the treatment I received. For it is not only against all reason and moral law, but even the legal codes of all civilized nations will condemn as wanton cruelty the punishment of individuals who, against their will and desire, have lost the free control of their actions. I know perfectly well that people will simply deny the truth of my statements, and that I have suffered in a manner described in these pages, but if asked for a reason for their disbelief I think they would find it extremely hard to give a satisfactory explanation. I was not condemned by reason and calm, impartial justice, but by passion and impulse, which saw only the effects of the crime, but was blind to its causes.

I think, after the first excitement was over, some of the fairer-minded and more intelligent people perceived that perhaps not all was right at my trial. But as it is the curse of the hasty, unjust action that it can only be remedied by an acknowledgment of the error and injustice committed, people much rather try to deceive themselves and others by every means in their power than admit having been guilty of an error of judgment.

It would be folly for me to look for justice, even at this late date, for the infamous

treatment I was accorded by those interested in my trial, and, considering the
abuse heaped upon me by the public press,
it would never do for them to admit that I
was not all they pictured me.

R. Holzhey[1]

---

[1] *Detroit Evening News,* November 27, 1893,
"A Mad Study."

Birth of a New Man

The surgery on my skull was successful. A bone fragment had been putting pressure on my brain, and its removal made me into a new man. I had a silver plate in my head and recovered sufficiently by the summer of 1894 to allow my return to the state prison in Marquette. Once again I took every opportunity to delve into the prison library and improve my knowledge. Many hours and days were spent engrossed in books, particularly on the topics of metaphysics and psychology.

Warden Van Evera appointed me prison librarian. I wrote for the *Progress*, a newspaper published at the prison. I was appointed official photographer of the prison and was responsible for taking mugshots of new prisoners when they arrived. Besides that I earned small sums of money by producing and selling glass souvenir paperweights. I became interested in studying the field of investing and tried my hand at investing in stocks. The warden helped me out by conducting all of the necessary transactions for me. After several years my investments proved a lucrative activity.

In the spring of 1896 I wrote a letter to the board of pardons, explaining my case in detail and requesting their advice.

Gentlemen:

Restrained by a remnant of pride (which refuses to ask justice or mercy from those that hate me—meaning the public you represent), and a bitter knowledge of human nature in some of its aspects (which pronounces it folly to do so), I have always abstained from applying for a pardon, although convinced that, from the nature and circumstances attending my misdeeds, there were good and substantial reasons to support such a claim.

Now, being aware of these things, on the other hand, I have been much troubled in my conscience with the idea that it was wrong and unmanly to submit passively and supinely to a judgment and treatment that, taking all things into consideration, I know to be unjust and inhuman, both from a legal and moral point of view. Then to achieve peace of mind, if nothing more, I should like to ask your opinion on certain points bearing on my case.

As you may know, I am charged with highway robbery and incidentally murder (although there is a strong doubt in my mind as to the latter), actuated, according to the prosecution, by greed—by the love of gold—and, perhaps, by malice and a desire for notoriety and similar base motives.

Now, on my part, I know and assert, that neither greed nor vainglory had the least to do with making me a criminal. That, in fact, I became such sorely against my will, through the pressure and perversions of nervous collapse and prostration, and that my whole criminal course consisted of the blind and fatal attempts of a morbid and tortured fancy, seeking to relieve a mental condition that had become unbearable, and which, in nine cases out of ten, amongst those similarly situated, would drive its victims to suicide or the lunatic asylum.

Whatever else my views may have been and I fully comprehend the facility of the human mind for self deception, yet of this much I am certain—that they were the direct effects of a protracted physical and nervous collapse, pure and simple, obscuring the reason and perverting judgment. Now the questions I should like to ask of you are these:

1. Taking for granted that I spoke the absolute truth concerning these matters, should I, in your opinion, be deserving of

a pardon, either on grounds
of justice, or mercy, or both,
or neither?

2. If your decisions do not, only in
   part, depend on the inherent mer-
   its of the case—on principle as
   perceived by you—but rather on
   unfavorable public sentiment—on
   the interest taken in the prisoner
   by outside parties, etc.; if such is
   the case, would I be allowed to
   make an appeal to this public sentiment, to men at large? For it
   seems to me one of the first principles of justice that the plea should
   be addressed to those on whom the
   decision and judgment depend.

If you will kindly grant a concise and
unambiguous answer to questions one and
two, you would greatly oblige, yours most
respectfully, *R. Holzhey.*

*P.S. I am asking you these questions
chiefly to ascertain if I have a case or not in
your opinion.*[2]

In 1898 I read in a newspaper that Otto Risum
had been charged with embezzlement of $80 while
serving as postmaster in Pulcifer. I thought about it

---

[2] *Ironwood Times,* 18 April 1896, "Holzhay's Appeal."

and decided to inform the authorities that this sum of money had been taken by me when I rifled the mail pouches during my second stagecoach robbery in 1889. The district attorney came up from Milwaukee to visit me in prison and took my deposition. Unless I had provided this information, Mr. Risum would have gone to prison.

I went before the board of pardons and requested a pardon, which was turned down. But a few more years of service as a model prisoner gained me more respect and supporters, and in the spring of 1904 Governor Bliss commuted one of my life sentences. My friends began efforts to have me pardoned, which took almost ten years to accomplish.

*Reimund Holzhey is the man seated
behind the table at right.
From the collection of the
Marquette County Historical Society.*

Appeal to the Public

On February 27, 1904 I once again felt compelled to tell my story to the public, so I sent the following letter to the *Houghton Mining Gazette*:

Marquette Prison

Your publication of February 17th contained an article headed "Holzhey's case" and which gave a rather graphic description as to how the seductive yellow-back novel lured that dubious character into the paths of crime in the days of his callow youth. Now so many imaginary stories, each one pretending to give the true reason why and wherefore I became an outlaw have been written that quite a bulky set of legends has grown up around my unfortunate self; but strange to relate, few, if any, ever included the actual, prosaic facts. According to the various versions I was urged on by a craving for notoriety; by the greed for gold, by the desire to obtain the means for a dissolute life; by pure deviltry; and now, according to the story of your informants, by the insidious "yellow backs." How would it be if I add one more, the true version of this growing mythos? It could do no harm, and I am somewhat curious to test that old saw about the final triumph of truth over men's airy fancies.

The Mining Gazette plainly writes in perfect good faith and with friendly intent; but when its informants described the writer as an exceptionally brilliant pupil, the leader of his class in school, they at once left the narrow realm of fact for the wider one of fiction, where their exuberant imagination could roam more at ease. If he had been as bright as depicted, his teachers and mates must have most shamefully conspired to conceal that happy fact from him, treating him always as a very ordinary and by no means over brilliant scholar. As to the demoralizing influence of the "Diamond Dick" kind of literature, it never casts its blight upon the subject of the sketch. The nearest approach to anything in this line he can remember reading, when about ten or twelve years old, were some translations of Cooper's "Leather Stocking Tales." Presumably as with most healthy, normal minded boys of that age, I may have experienced some longing then for a life of adventure in those delightful sylvan solitudes where the noble red man, yearning for pale face scalps, roamed at large. Nevertheless, to hold good, old Fenimore Cooper, and the delicious thrills he may have inspired in my childish breast at that time, responsible for the queerish deeds committed by me more than ten years later would certainly be doing the old gentleman a grave injustice.

It would lead too far to demonstrate in detail the innate inconsistencies and absurdities of the many stories that have been published setting forth why I became a criminal. Let one suffice. Does a moment's reflection not show that should a young man of twenty-two, supposing him to be in his right mind, suddenly set out to mold himself upon a "Nick Carter" model, his intellect must necessarily be of an infantile, semi-idiotic kind, too stupid to draw a line between fact and fancy? A mind so dense and silly at that age would in all probability largely remain so to the end of the chapter, because lacking in the very first principles of good sense and reason, of which, according to all reports, I was not denied a fair share.

But instead of wasting space with mere refutations, I had perhaps better come to the point by stating a few of the salient facts of my life and the actual causes which really did lead to so much trouble to myself, as well as to others. I was born and educated in Germany, coming to this country when between fifteen and sixteen years of

age. For the succeeding seven years, except-
ing a few short intervals, including a trip to
the lumber regions of the Pacific coast, I
worked steadily in various branches of the
lumber industry in Wisconsin—no better,
no worse man than most others. Then came
the crash—sudden, inexplicable to friends
and onlookers—though not quite to myself.

For a year or more I had been in a state
of continuous ill-health. None of your plain
and obvious live or die diseases, but simply
an aggravated nerve-shattering form of
dyspepsia and insomnia; the latter, towards
the end, putting sleep wholly out of the
question. Of course, under such conditions
mental depression, melancholia and curious
freak ideas and morbid impulses came on
apace, which gradually entirely transformed and finally subverted my normal
self. Nevertheless it would have taken a
close and experienced observer to notice
this inward change, which even to close
associates could only have shown itself in
an increasingly gloomy and morbid disposition and temper. Confidants as to my conditions, I had none. Indeed I was far from
clearly realizing the nature of the case
myself, much less foreseeing subsequent
events. Thus for a long time I kept to
myself, outwardly, indifferently well in
hand; but finally the indescribable mental
strain consequent upon physical nervous
collapse reached the breaking point, and
out of the resulting nervous mental crisis

emerged, meteor-like, the terrible and villainous "Black Bart" of popular conception.

The world quite naturally saw but an evil-minded, wanton desperado, or else a witless "would be" dime novel hero; but in reality that spectacular "terror" was for the time being simply a most melancholy, half-crazed sort of an idiot, seeking instinctively relief from unbearable distress in a series of senseless, foolhardy exploits.

Ordinarily men conditioned as I was either become suicides or full-fledged lunatics. Fortunately, or unfortunately, my mind was of too robust a constitution to break down completely. It became excessively morbid, warped, distorted, but it refused to go into a total eclipse. For a time I wandered in the misty borderland where sanity and insanity meet. A few freak ideas and impulses became with me the dominant factors of consciousness, all else sinking gradually out of sight. Stronger than all arose an irresistible desire for actions involving extreme hazard and danger, and, strangely enough, the sensation of imminent peril, of facing possible death and disaster, always acted like a powerful soothing tonic upon my overwrought mind. It broke down the spell of distressing, self-centered thought and, instinctively, without forethought or clear realization, I drifted from one foolhardy exploit to another in order to maintain the relief giving nervous tension accruing from such conduct. There was no intent or desire to harm others; there was no deep laid plots to gather in riches; for no man possessing the mere rudiments of common sense would have tried to do so by such blundering, foolish deeds as were mine. Moreover, it was months after all was over, and not until I had finally recovered, that I myself came to a clear realization as to the nature of my own previous condition. Such being the case it is not to be wondered at that men should have misjudged my case, ascribing my misdoings to all kinds of outlandish and sinister motives. Truth is, people, even my associates and acquaintances were probably rather non-plussed and at a loss to explain my sudden blooming forth into an ultra reckless desperado and, not knowing the real reason why and wherefore, they jumped at several kinds of conclusions, which have ever since passed as proven facts.

The above are in a bare outline the actual facts of "Holzhey's case," giving the cause and reason why once upon a time he became a highly spectacular, sensational desperado. The love of notoriety, "yellow back" novels, evil associations, dissipation or the shear greed of gold did not enter into the problem. It was first and last a case of physical, and consequent nervous-mental, demoralization, nothing more and nothing less. This version of the case will bear investigation—the more of it the better. It will be found to cover the case in detail as well as in its more general aspects.

Is it not passing strange that a person should lead an ordinary, non-criminal life up to a certain point, then suddenly, without apparent rhyme or reason, burst forth into a series of furious antics (committed without and within prison)—later on ceasing almost as abruptly as they began—except there was behind it all some unusual, special cause? Can any man live for fourteen years under the soul searching conditions of prison life and show no sign of a criminal or violent disposition, if the latter were part and parcel of his real nature? The perfect hypocrite, never falling out of his role, never was nor ever will be. Had I really been the naturally witless, or violent and villainous character often pictured is it likely I could have completely sloughed off and transformed my old self in the space of a few months, coming forth a peaceful, rational and well disposed human being, as I may claim to have been these dozen years or more.

A temporary abnormal and morbid state of mind does explain and cover my case and conduct in all its bearings. This story, moreover, is borne out by a multitude of facts and plain deductions. Nevertheless the writer is not in the least sanguine that his version of "Holzhey's case" will ever become very popular. It is altogether too

tame and non-sensational and, worse than
all, entirely lacking in that delightful ele-
ment of deliberate deviltry, of native
wickedness, average human nature is so
fond of imagining as actuating the conduct
of "others." But yet, truth does have a peculiar knack of slowly worming its way up
through mountains of super-imposed false-
hoods, and it is just possible that, ulti-
mately, it will find its way to the light in
this case also.

R. Holzhey[3]

*Nameplate used on back of Holzhey's photographs.
Courtesy of Marquette County Historical Society.*

[3] *Ironwood News Record,* March 12, 1904, "Holzhey's
Life Story."

My Rehabilitation

During my long incarceration at Marquette I had access to the prison library and delved into many topics, including history. German history was one of my favorite subjects. Ever since my childhood in Germany I had been fascinated by the story of the ancient German military leader Arminius who defeated Caesar's army in the Teutoburg Forest in 9 A.D. This legendary event was taught to us in school and the lesson reinforced by the conflicts between the Germans and Napoleon's armies in the early 19th century and again in 1870-71.

I often fancied myself to be a descendant of those Teutonic tribesmen led by "Hermann;" our surname Holzhey meant 'one descended from the forest dwellers' in Old German. Perhaps this explains my hunting and fishing skills and my ability to survive in the woods. This conflict between the Teutons and the Latins had a powerful effect on the German psyche; I once told a newspaper reporter that the Milwaukee &

Northern train I robbed back in 1889 had no men aboard—only Italians!

*Holzhey is the man in the center,
resting his hand on the table.
Collection of Superior View, Marquette.*

My fellow inmates referred to me as the "professor." I was writing stories for newspapers and taking care of my investments so that I would have a means of support should I ever be released from prison. I felt I needed to convince the public that I was neither a raving lunatic nor a hardened criminal. My goal was to secure a pardon and begin to live a normal life. In 1911 Governor Warner commuted my sentence from life down to forty years, making me eligible for a pardon. At that time I sent another letter to the newspaper to try to explain my actions:

Marquette Prison

Of course, while Governor Warner's kindly act of commuting my sentence and paroling me has not been quite unexpected, still I had built no great expectations upon the possibility of my release. To one in my situation, building castles in the air is a rather unhealthy occupation, they are so prone to come crashing down about one's ears, so I gave up that practice years ago, making up my mind to meet both good and evil fortune with equanimity.

Without the slightest desire for it, much notoriety has come my way in the past, and the things said and written about me were usually a curious mixture of fact and fancy. Because my case had somewhat unusual and peculiar features about it, all sorts of constructions were placed upon it, and me, to explain the why and whyfore of my actions, but never the right one, for that was far too simple and obvious. I was pictured as a bold, bad man, a would-be dime novel hero, and what not. But the bald truth at the root of my troubles was merely a physical-nervous breakdown at the critical age of adolescence, a depressed and highly morbid state of mind, with the will temporarily under the sway of abnormal ideas and notions leading for the time being to actions which were wholly at variance with my normal self, before and since. Of course justice, as yet, is not trained to see the underlying causes and motives. It takes the evil deed and ascribes the most sinister motive which will best aid conviction, and let it go at that. I was not in a condition then to explain matters, having but a confused realization of the facts myself, and, moreover, even if properly set forth, my explanation would have met with nothing but ridicule as a disingenuous device to escape punishment.

Twenty-one years have passed away since then, and it is gratifying to note that at last the world has come to the conclusion that crime is often the result of causes and conditions of which the transgressor himself is the victim, and that, on the whole, his reform and redemption is better than the vengeful punishment and retaliation of the supposed good old times, which too often managed to transform the chance offender into a habitual one—envenomed and vindictive.

As to myself, I have been treated with the utmost fairness during the last four administrations, which cover the last twenty years. I have been the prison librarian and photographer for about seventeen years, practically since the inception of those departments. As to the future, I have not given it much thought, but shall take up whatever comes to hand to make a living.

I am profoundly grateful to Governor Warner for his clemency in my case, as well as to Warden Russell and the gentlemen who interested themselves in my case. The very least I can do on my part to show my appreciation of their kindness is to live the remainder of my days an upright and honorable life in the active world to which the clemency of the governor has restored me.

R. Holzhey[4]

---

[4] *Ironwood News Record,* January 7, 1911, "Holzhey To Be Freed."

A Free Man!

The long-awaited day finally arrived. Just after midnight on July 7, 1913, I got into a coach driven by the Reverend G. Bates Burt of Marquette, an Episcopal minister. I hid beneath the seat to escape the attention of the crowd of reporters who were waiting outside to see me. That night I stayed in the Reverend's home on Ridge street, and the next morning I boarded the train at the Pine street crossing in the city and went to Big Bay. John Longyear had agreed to hire me as a cook's helper at Longyear Farm on Ives lake. This was my first full day as a free man, and I wanted to spend it alone, enjoying the sunset, the open air and the stars in the night sky, so I stayed out on the Point until the sun rose the next day.

I purchased a Goerz Tenax folding camera and took many photographs in my spare time on Longyear Farm. After about a year, I decided it was time to go into business for myself, so I rented a building at 301 south Front street in Marquette, and opened up a photographic studio, living upstairs. I assumed the alias "Carl Paul" soon after my release and was known by that name during all of the period of my residence in Marquette county. My inspiration for using this name was a fellow German, Carl Paul Goerz, who founded the C. P. Goerz American Optical Company, producers of fine cameras. Goerz had a lense- grinding factory in Thuringia.

But somehow my true identity became known, and business suffered as a consequence. Once again the Longyears came to my aid, and I was allowed to live on the property of the Huron Mountain Club, where I moved my studio and equipment. There I worked as a fishing guide and sold photographs to the tourists.

Paul Carl, photogr 301 S Front, res same
Paull Frank O phys Frei blk res 343 E N

Holzhey was listed under an alias
in the 1916-17 Polk Directory.

An imaginative photograph of uncertain origin,
acquired in Marquette, "in the style of" Carl Paul,
circa 1915. Note the revolver sitting
on the tree stump.

About 1917 I decided to travel out West and see Yellowstone National Park. I spent some time there taking nature photographs and selling them to tourists, none of whom were acquainted with my past history. It was a different and pleasant kind of experience to deal with people who had formed no prejudices against me and knew me only as the honorable and upright man that I was. This business was conducted for a season, and then I returned to the Huron Mountain Club and secured a position as guard on the Salmon Trout, living in a log cabin near the forks of the river.

Many stories went around concerning my career and financial affairs. There were rumors floating around about me going down to Shawano county to recover stolen money and loot. A few eyebrows were raised when I purchased a large life insurance policy; a transaction made possible by my stock market investments. When the crash came in 1929, old age was approaching, and I decided to move to Florida in order to cut my expenses and escape those who still thought ill of me. In Florida, I felt, I would stand a better chance of living out my life in security.

In 1932 I bought a place on Captiva Island, off Fort Myers. Two years later I purchased my present home. I returned to the Huron Mountain Club every summer to see my old friends until old age began to get the better of me. Here I have my typewriter and books and spend my time reading and writing. I rent cottages to the tourists and sometimes shoot the wild cats roaming around my property. My stories are sold to magazines and newspapers and help keep food on my table.

And so this is my life's story. I am now eighty-five years old and my health is in serious decline. I have no relatives in this country with the exception of one cousin. Clara comes over everyday to make my meals and check on me. I spend long periods sitting on the porch in back of my home, thinking. The world has gone to hell during my lifetime. My old homeland was destroyed in the war, my boyhood home is now part of a communist state, and the threat of nuclear destruction hangs over the earth. I do not think I am long for this world.

FORT MYERS NEWS-PRESS

FORT MYERS, FLA., FRIDAY, SEPTEMBER 26, 1952

Neighbor Finds Suicide's Body

Aged Sanibel Writer Kills Self On Porch

*Reimund Holzhey apparently drew this picture of two
running horses and/or used it in his glass paperweights, which he signed on the bottom side. Courtesy
of Ironwood Carnegie Library.*

Sources

Ashland Daily News
Ashland Daily Press

Cowdery, Mike, "Reimund Holzhey &
   The Gogebic Stage Robbery," in North
   Country Folk Publications, October
   1981. This was a mostly imaginary
   account of Holzhey, from his robbery
   of the stagecoach to his death.

Duluth Daily News
Detroit Evening News

Gogebic County Court Records
Gogebic County Vital Statistics
Gogebic Iron Tribune
Green Bay State Gazette
Green Bay State Daily

Ionia Standard
Ironwood Daily Globe
Ironwood News Record
Ironwood Times
Ishpeming Mining Journal

Lee County, Florida, Vital Statistics
Lemmer, Victor F., Collection, at Bentley
    Historical Library, University of
    Michigan, Box 7, Folder 7-14.

Marquette Mining Journal
Milwaukee Sentinel
Milwaukee Sunday Sentinel
Minneapolis Pioneer Press

Partridge, Scott, "The Bad Guy of Goge-
    bic," in *Detroit Free Press*, 24 June
    1984, is a good account of Holzhey's
    stagecoach robbery and capture.

Prison Records

Rydholm, Fred, *Superior Heartland, A
    Backwoods History* (Marquette, Mi.:
    Fred Rydholm, 1989), 567-70, carries
    an interesting account of Holzhey,
    with details on his life while living in
    Marquette after his release from
    prison.

Shawano County Journal

United States Census Records

Index

Holzhey, Reimund,

Holzhey, Reimund,

Printed in the United States
99968LV00001B/184-345/A

9 781598 583465